# Sea Life Alphabet
## Coloring Book

### Ruth Soffer

Dover Publications, Inc.
Mineola, New York

*Bibliographical Note*

*Sea Life Alphabet Coloring Book* is a new work, first published by
Dover Publications, Inc., in 2003.

*International Standard Book Number*

*ISBN-13: 978-0-486-42653-2*
*ISBN-10: 0-486-42653-X*

Manufactured in the United States by Courier Corporation
42653X08    2015
www.doverpublications.com

## PUBLISHER'S NOTE

Beneath the surface of the world's oceans lies an immense and varied realm of sea life, including fish, kelp, coral, jellyfish, octopi, sea horses, urchins, crabs, sea snakes, and many other denizens of the deep. This coloring book offers not only an opportunity to learn to recognize and identify a rich cross-section of these fascinating creatures, but allows you a chance to bring your coloring abilities into play as you recreate the rainbow hues of life beneath the waves. Additionally, young colorists will reinforce letter and word recognition skills as they have fun coloring.

**A is for Anemone**

Anemone Clownfish (*Amphiprion bicinctus*). Anemone (*Radianthus ritteri*).

**B is for Butterflyfish**

*Top left*: Lemon Butterflyfish (*Chaetodon miliaris*). *Top right*: Longsnout Butterflyfish (*Forcipiger longirostris*). *Bottom*: Ornamented Butterflyfish (*Chaetodon ornatissimus*). Broccoli Coral (*Alcyonium* sp.)

**C is for Clingfish**
Doubleline Clingfish (*Lepadichthys lineatus*). Yellow Crinoid (*Comanthina*).

**D is for Dolphin**

Bottlenose Dolphin (*Tursiops truncatus*). Atlantic Spotted Dolphin (*Stenella plagiodon*).

**E is for Emperor Angelfish**
(*Pomacanthus imperator*)

**F is for Filefish**

*Top and center*: Fringed Filefish (*Monacanthus ciliatus*). *Bottom left*: Frillfin Goby (*Bathygobius soporator*).  Fire Coral (*Millepora complanta*).

**G is for Grouper**

Grouper (*Cephalopholis miniatus*). Gorgonian Coral (*Dendronephthya*).

**H is for Hawkfish**

Hawkfish (*Cirrhitichthys oxycephalus*). Antler Coral (*Pocillopora eydouxi*).

**I is for Indigo Hamlet**
(*Hypoplectrus indigo*)

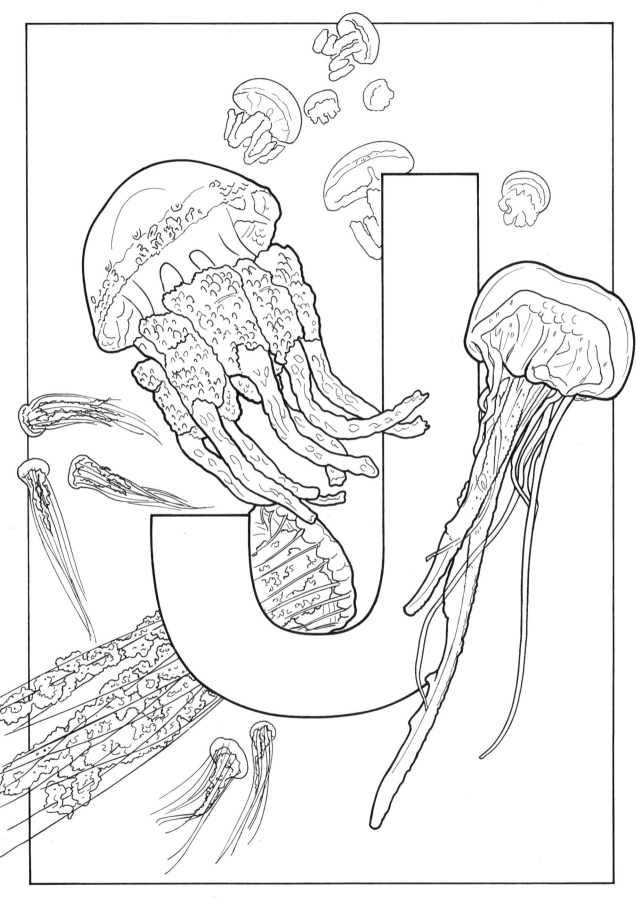

**J is for Jellyfish**

*Far right*: Purple Jellyfish (*Pelagia noctiluca*). *Bottom left*: Sea Nettle (*Chrysaora fuscescens*).
*Left center*: Papuan Jellyfish (*Mastigias papua*).

**K is for Kelp**

Kelp Forest, Monterey Bay, California. Harbor Seal (*Phoca vitulina concolor*).

**L is for Lionfish**
(*Pterois volitans*)

**Caribbean Reef**

(See page 32 for key to illustration)

**M is for Moorish Idol**
(*Zanclus cornutus*)

**N is for Nudibranchs**

Top left: *Glossodoris Californiensis.* Top right: *Chromodoris coi.* Center: Purple (*Chromodoris* sp.).
Bottom: *Laila cockerelli*

**O is for Octopus**
Giant Pacific (*Octopus dolfleini*)

**P is for Parrotfish**

Parrotfish (*Scarus* sp.). Fire Coral (*Millepora* sp.).

**Q is for Queen Angelfish**

*Top and center*: Adult Queen Angelfish (*Holacanthus ciliaris*).
*Bottom*: Juvenile Queen Angelfish.

**R is for Red Lizardfish**

*Top*: Red Lizardfish (*Synodus synodus*). *Center*: Reef Squirrelfish (*Sargocentron coruscus*).
*Bottom*: Red Hind (*Epinephelus guttatus*).

**S is for Sea Horse**

Large Sea Horse (*Hippocampus reidi*). Small Sea Horse (*Hippocampus* sp.).
Gorgonian Coral.

**T is for Triggerfish**

Triggerfish (*Pseudobalistes fuscus*). Tube Coral (*Tubastrea micrantha*).

**U is for Urchin**

*Left and mid right*: Long-spined Sea Urchin (*Diadema antillarum*). *Front right and background*: Atlantic Purple Sea Urchin (*Arbacia punctulata*).

**V is for Vermilion Snapper**

Vermilion Snapper (*Rhomboplites aurorubens*). *Background*: Tubular sponges (*Verongia* sp.).
Foreground: *Verongia longissima*

**W is for Wrasse**

*Top and background*: Creole Wrasse (*Clepticus parrae*).
*Bottom*: Bluehead Wrasse (*Thalassoma bifasciatum*).

**X is for Xanthid Crab**
(*Leptodius exaratus*)

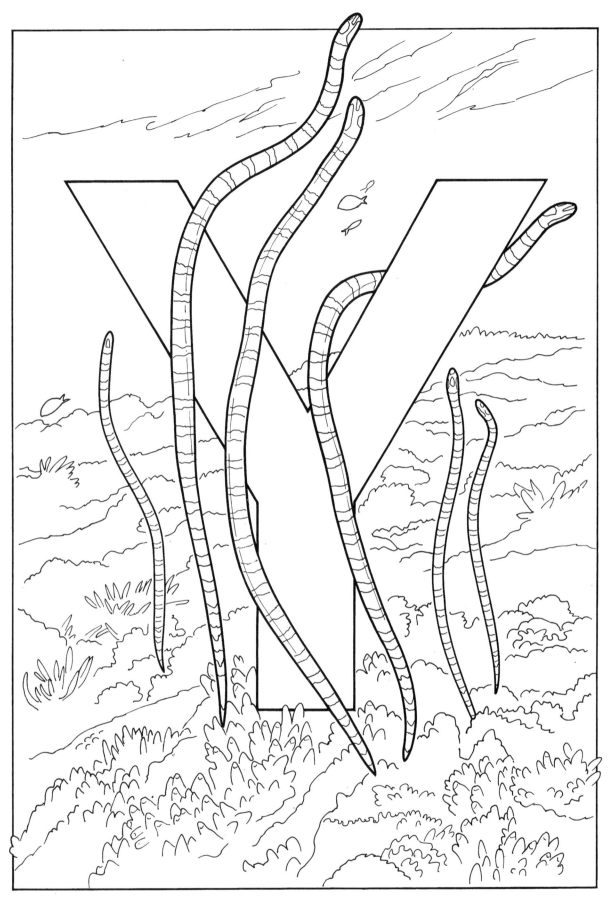

**Y is for Yellow-lip Sea Snake**
(*Laticauda colubrina*)

**Z is for Ziebell's Handfish**
(*Brachionichthys* sp.)

## Key to Caribbean Reef (pp. 16–17)

1. Gorgonian Coral
   (*Plexaura flexuosa*)
2. Gorgonian Coral (*Plexaura* sp.)
3. Green Sea Turtle
   (*Chelonia mydas*)
4. Loggerhead Turtle
   (*Caretta caretta*)

5. Caribbean Sharpnose Shark
   (*R. porosus*)
6. Blue Shark (*Prionace glauca*)
7. Yellowtail Snapper
   (*Ocyurus chrysurus*)

8. Barred Hamlet
   (*Hypoplectrus puella*)
9. Stoplight Parrotfish
   (*Sparisoma viride*)
10. Yellowtail Damselfish
    (*Microspathodon chrysurus*)

11. Spotted Moray
    (*Gymnothorax moringa*)
12. Indigo Hamlet
    (*Hypoplectrus indigo*)
13. Gorgonian Sea Fan
    (*Corynactis californica*)